All about Our Earth

Planet Earth remains mankind's only home and resource, the most baffling and complex mechanism in the universe. A simple and informative text backed by lavish full-color artwork lays bare the secrets of continental drift, volcanic eruption, weather systems, oceanography and many more aspects of the natural forces that rule our lives.

Contents

How the Earth was made

Our planet Earth is one of the nine planets which rotate around the Sun in the solar system. The Sun, a medium-sized star, is only one of millions in the Milky Way galaxy. Beyond our galaxy, the universe contains millions of other galaxies.

How was our solar system created? Scientists have put forward several theories. One theory suggests that a star once passed close to our Sun. Because of gravity, a streamer of gas and dust would have been torn from the star and the Sun. As this material rotated around the Sun, it would have collected together to form the planets, moons and other bodies in the solar system. Few scientists, however, think that this is a likely theory.

A second theory suggests that the Sun was once much bigger than it is today and that it was spinning around quickly. As it spun, it may have ejected a cloud of gas and dust, which later formed the planets. This is a

fairly new and untested theory.

The third and most popular theory is that the solar system was formed from a vast cloud of dust and gas that was drifting through space. At the center of this cloud, the dust and gas were drawn together to form a hot mass, which became the Sun. Then the remaining material came together to form the planets.

The age of the Earth

People once thought that the Earth was formed recently. In the 1600s, a scholar, Bishop Ussher, added up all the generations of people in the Bible. He worked out that the Earth was created on October 23, 4004 BC.

However, in the 1800s, scientists realized that the Earth must be many millions of years old. In the early 1900s, ways of measuring the ages of rocks were discovered. The oldest rocks yet found on Earth are more than 3,700,000,000 years old. But the solar system itself is much older than this. Meteors have been found that are about 4,550,000,000 years old and, recently, some Moon rocks have been dated at 4,600,000,000 years. We now believe that this is the age of the Earth.

Rocks formed in the first 900 million years of Earth history have probably been destroyed.

After it had formed, the Earth was a blazing hot planet, covered by molten rock. Huge volcanic explosions threw up lighter substances to form the thin crust. Beneath the crust lay denser substances in the mantle and the core. The core is four to five times as dense as the crust and probably consists mostly of iron and nickel.

The air around the Earth

The crust was constantly cracked and re-melted and gases were released from the rocks. These gases formed a poisonous atmosphere, containing little oxygen. Water vapor was also released from the rocks when volcanoes erupted. The water vapor formed clouds and, finally, rain fell to the surface during great storms. As the surface cooled, water collected in hollows to form the first seas.

In these seas, chemical reactions occurred, which created the first living cells. The oldest known living things were primitive plants, growing about 3,100,000,000 years ago. Much later in Earth history, around 1,900,000,000

Below: Molten lava pours from a volcano at Surtsey, an island off Iceland, in 1964. In the early days of Earth history, the entire surface of the Earth was probably molten, with a temperature of more than 1000°C.

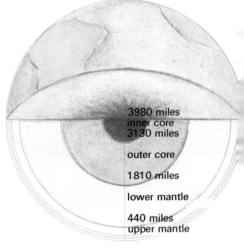

3980 miles	inner core
3130 miles	
outer core	
1810 miles	
lower mantle	
440 miles	
upper mantle	

THE EARTH'S INTERIOR

Above: It is about 3980 miles from the Earth's surface to its center. The continental crust has a maximum thickness of 40–45 miles. The ocean crust, which also underlies the continents, is only about 4 miles thick. Beneath it is the mantle, which encloses the core. The outer core is liquid, but the inner core is solid.

years ago, advanced plants evolved. They produced life-giving oxygen, which steadily increased in the air, making it breathable. Some oxygen high up in the atmosphere was changed by the Sun's radiation into a gas called ozone. Ozone blocks out most of the Sun's harmful ultraviolet rays. Without oxygen and ozone, life on Earth would be impossible.

Right: The solar system probably formed from a vast cloud of gas and dust (1), which was drifting through space. Because of gravity, the particles were drawn together and the cloud grew smaller. Because it was rotating, the cloud was also flattened into a disk. Heavier particles were drawn together towards the center. There they formed a large central mass (2). This extremely hot central mass developed into the Sun, while the rest of the material in the surrounding disk formed the planets (3). Today, our solar system consists of nine planets and other bodies which rotate around the Sun (4). Our Earth is the third planet from the Sun.

Below: This photograph of the Earth from space shows most of Africa and Arabia at the top. At the bottom is the icy continent of Antarctica. The oceans are partly covered by clouds.

Right: The diagram shows an edge-on view of the Milky Way galaxy. It contains millions of stars arranged in a central hub with spiral arms. Our solar system is two-thirds of the way out from the central hub. The distance across the Milky Way galaxy is about 100,000 light years. One light year is about 5.9 trillion miles.

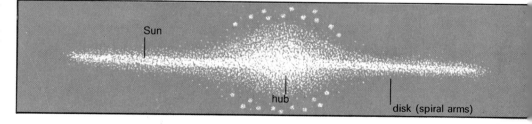

Sun

hub

disk (spiral arms)

3

The atmosphere

The atmosphere is a blanket of air surrounding the Earth. If the Earth did not have a protective atmosphere, the Sun's rays would scorch our planet during the day, and temperatures would plummet far below freezing at night.

The composition of air

By volume, dry air consists mostly of three gases: nitrogen (78.09 per cent), oxygen (20.95 per cent) and argon (0.93 per cent). The other 0.03 per cent consists of such gases as carbon dioxide, helium, hydrogen, krypton, methane, neon, ozone and xenon. The lowest layer of the atmosphere, called the *troposphere*, also contains water vapor. The amount of water vapor is quite small, varying from one to four per cent.

In some areas, dust, smoke and harmful gases enter the air from factories or from the exhaust pipes of cars. Nuclear explosions also throw radioactive particles and gases into the air. All these substances pollute the air, even when they are present in very small amounts. Air pollution is a serious hazard to health and may also damage metals and stonework. Today many countries have laws to control air pollution.

Air pressure

Clean air is invisible, tasteless and odorless, but the atmosphere weighs an estimated 5000 trillion tons. This means that a column of air weighing about 1 ton is pressing down on your shoulders. The effect of air pressure can be shown by pumping all the air from a can, creating a vacuum inside it. The air then presses onto the can, making it crumple and collapse. We do not notice air pressure, because the pressure inside our bodies is the same as the air pressure on the outside.

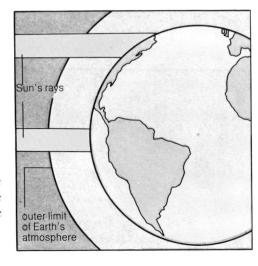

Belwo: A cloud of smog hangs over Santiago, a city in Chile. Smog, a word which comes from "smoky fog," is often caused by dirt and gases poured into the air by coal fires in homes or by furnaces in factories. Another kind of smog is caused largely by car exhaust fumes. The most unpleasant effects of smog are felt when polluted air lingers for some time over the land. Industrial and car exhaust gases are usually carried away by rising air currents. But they are sometimes trapped by a process called temperature inversion. This occurs when the ground is chilled. The air near the ground then becomes colder and heavier than the warmer air above it. Hence, polluted air around ground level is trapped and cannot rise.

Above: The amount of heat that reaches the Earth's surface varies between the poles and the equator. Around the poles, the Sun's rays pass through a greater thickness of atmosphere. The atmosphere absorbs heat, so less heat reaches the surface at the poles than at the equator. Near the poles, the Sun's rays also spread over a large area, hence, the poles get less heat than do tropical regions.

Below: Mountaineers often wear oxygen masks when climbing high peaks. This is because the air becomes thinner, or more rarefied, the higher one goes above sea level. Rarefied air is also a problem for athletes from low-lying countries who compete in games held in places on high plateaus.

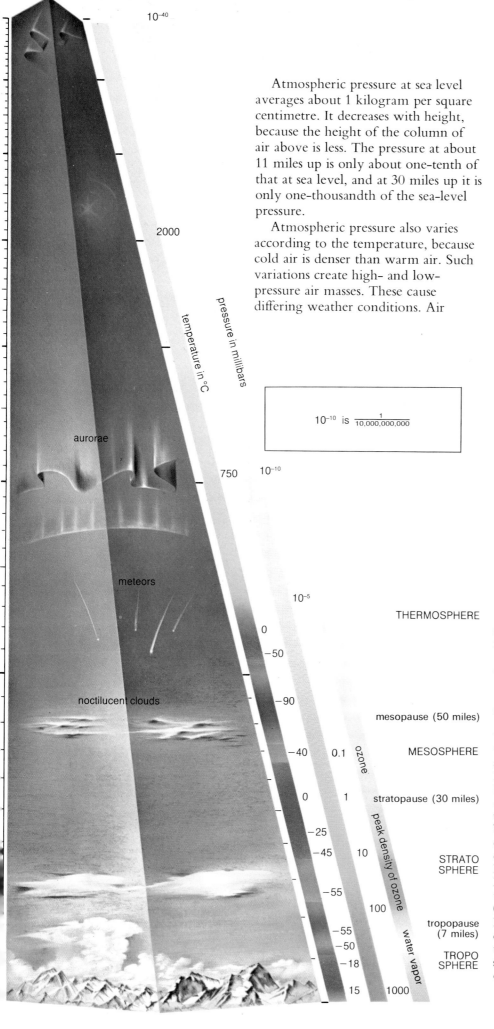

Atmospheric pressure at sea level averages about 1 kilogram per square centimetre. It decreases with height, because the height of the column of air above is less. The pressure at about 11 miles up is only about one-tenth of that at sea level, and at 30 miles up it is only one-thousandth of the sea-level pressure.

Atmospheric pressure also varies according to the temperature, because cold air is denser than warm air. Such variations create high- and low-pressure air masses. These cause differing weather conditions. Air pressure is measured by instruments called barometers, in units called millibars. A pressure of 1000 millibars is roughly the same as an air pressure which can support a 30-inch column of mercury.

Layers of the atmosphere

About 80 percent of the mass of the atmosphere is in its lowest layer, the troposphere. On average, the troposphere is about 7 miles high. Its height varies from 11 miles above the equator to 5 miles over the poles.

In the troposphere, the temperature decreases with height, by roughly 11°C for every mile. Temperatures become stable at about −55°C at the top of the troposphere. This level is called the *tropopause*.

Above the tropopause is the *stratosphere*. Temperatures remain the same for the bottom 6 miles of the stratosphere. But they then rise until, at about 30 miles up, the *stratopause* is reached. Above this level lie the other two zones of the atmosphere, the *mesosphere* and the *thermosphere*, which are separated by the *mesopause*. This thermosphere gradually decreases in density until it fades into space.

Left: The layers of the atmosphere are the troposphere, stratosphere, mesosphere and thermosphere. The troposphere contains about 80 per cent of the air in the atmosphere, and nearly all the water vapor. The diagram shows that temperatures fall steadily with height until they reach −55°C at the top of the troposphere, which is the tropopause. Above the tropopause is the stratosphere. Jet aircraft fly in the lower stratosphere. But the stratosphere is important because of its layer of ozone. This ozone filters out the Sun's harmful ultraviolet rays. The mesosphere, between 30 and 50 miles high, contains noctilucent clouds. These consist of dust from meteors which have burned up while approaching Earth. Above the mesosphere is the thermosphere. This contains only 0.001 per cent of the atmosphere. Disturbances in the thermosphere, caused by streams of particles from the Sun, create glowing lights in the sky, called aurorae. Artificial satellites orbit the Earth in the thermosphere.

Winds and weather

Winds are large-scale movements of air. The chief factor which causes air to move is heat from the Sun.

The main wind systems

The Sun's heat is most intense around the equator. There, the air is heated and rises in fast-moving upward air currents. This is because warm air is lighter (less dense) than cool air.

Because the air is rising, the air pressure at the surface is reduced. This creates a low-pressure air belt, called the *doldrums*, which extends around the Earth. Air from the north and south is sucked into the doldrums to replace the rising air. This incoming air forms the *trade winds*.

The warm rising air cools high up in the troposphere, spreads out and then flows north and south. Eventually it sinks down around latitudes 30° north and 30° south. These regions, called the *horse latitudes*, are high-pressure zones. To relieve the pressure, winds blow outward. Some blow toward the equator in the trade winds. Others flow poleward in the *westerlies*. At the poles, the air is cold and dense. It moves away from the poles in winds called the *polar easterlies*.

Winds do not flow in a straight north–south direction. Instead, they are deflected by the rotation of the Earth. This effect is similar to what happens if you try to draw a straight line from north to south on a spinning globe. When the globe stops, you will see that you have drawn a curved line.

The world's main wind systems are shown on the map on page 7. But other factors complicate wind systems. Most important is the fact that land heats up and cools down faster than the oceans. Hence, in summer, air over tropical lands is heated faster than air over the seas. Intense heating of the land may create low-pressure air masses which draw in cooler air from the sea. Sometimes, wind directions are reversed between summer and winter; these are called *monsoons*.

Weather systems

There are two main kinds of weather systems. *Anticyclones* are high-pressure systems, in which air is descending. They generally have stable weather conditions. *Cyclones*, or *depressions*, are low-pressure systems, where warm air rises. Depressions have changeable weather.

Depressions form in the middle latitudes, where the polar easterlies meet the warm westerlies along the so-called *polar front*. Here, the cold and warm air are mixed. Depressions are rotating air masses, with warm, low-pressure air at their centers. The cold, denser air flows around the warm air, gradually forcing it upward and cooling it. The passage of a depression is marked by squally and rainy weather. Storms associated with depressions are called *cyclonic storms*.

Thunderstorms are other common storms. They occur when fast-rising warm air currents create cumulo-nimbus clouds (see page 8) Features of thunderstorms include thunder, lightning and heavy rain or snow.

North and south of the equator, destructive storms called hurricanes occur. These are large rotating air masses, with extremely low air pressures. Howling winds swirl around hurricanes, doing much damage.

Tornadoes are other destructive storms with even lower air pressures than hurricanes. Tornadoes are small in area, measuring less than one-third of a mile across, but their winds can rip trees out of the ground.

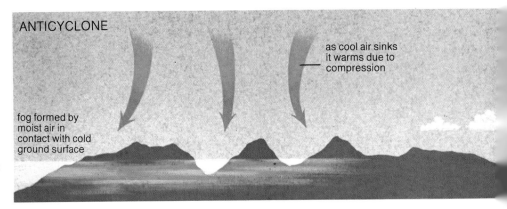

ANTICYCLONE

as cool air sinks it warms due to compression

fog formed by moist air in contact with cold ground surface

Below: A tornado on the plains. Tornadoes form when a funnel-like column of cold air sinks down from a storm cloud. Warm air rises, whirls around it and causes fierce winds.

Below right: This space photograph shows a hurricane off the coast of Cuba. The spiraling clouds show that the air is rotating rapidly around the center, or eye, of the hurricane.

Right: The map shows the Earth's main wind belts. Trade winds are shown in brown and purple, westerlies in green, and polar easterlies in blue. Other winds, shown in red, are caused by local factors, including the unequal heating of the land and sea.

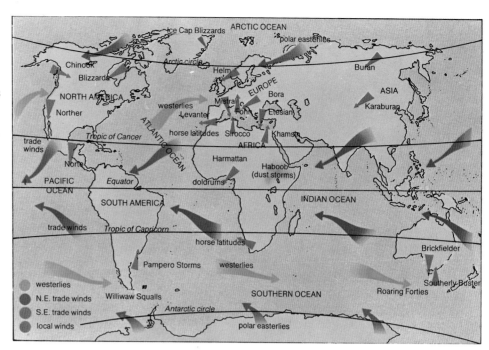

Below: Anticyclones, left, form when cool air sinks down, creating a high-pressure system, with stable weather conditions. Depressions, right, form when warm air mixes with cold air. On the left, cold air is pushing under the warm air along the cold front. As the warm air rises, cumulonimbus clouds form and heavy rain falls. On the right, warm air is forced up over the cold air along the warm front. Again, clouds form, but there is usually less rain.

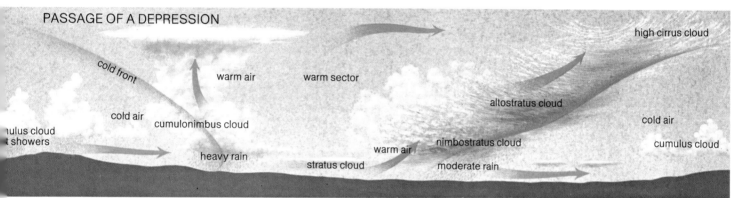

PASSAGE OF A DEPRESSION

high cirrus cloud

cold front

warm air

warm sector

altostratus cloud

cold air

cumulus cloud showers

cold air

cumulonimbus cloud

heavy rain

warm air

nimbostratus cloud

cumulus cloud

stratus cloud

moderate rain

Below right: The diagram shows how a hurricane is structured. At the center, or eye, of the hurricane, air is sinking downward. Here, calm weather conditions occur and there are no clouds in the sky. Around the eye, warm air is rising and storm clouds are forming. Also, the air is rotating in a spiral, creating strong, swirling winds. Winds in hurricanes may reach speeds of nearly 200 miles per hour. Hurricanes form in tropical regions over the oceans. When they move over land, they leave a trail of great destruction behind them.

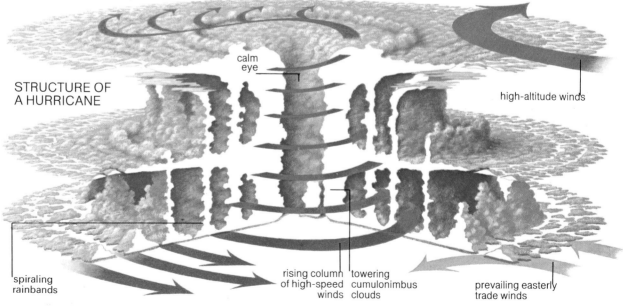

STRUCTURE OF A HURRICANE

calm eye

high-altitude winds

spiraling rainbands

rising column of high-speed winds

towering cumulonimbus clouds

prevailing easterly trade winds

Clouds

About 97.2 per cent of all the water in the world is in the oceans and 2.15 per cent is frozen in ice sheets and glaciers. Most of the rest is on land, either in rivers or lakes, or within the soil and rocks. Only 0.001 per cent of the world's water is airborne, but this moisture is vital for all animals and plants that live on land.

Water vapor and clouds

The Sun's heat evaporates water from the oceans. Evaporated water, or *water vapor*, is a dry, invisible substance, just like a gas. Water vapor is carried upward into the atmosphere by rising air currents.

Warm air can hold more water vapor than cold air. In fact, the hot air over deserts may contain more water vapor than cold air over temperate regions. When air contains all the water vapor it can hold at a given temperature, called the *dew point*, it is saturated. Saturated air has a *relative humidity* of 100 per cent. Relative humidity is a measure of the amount of water vapor in air, as a percentage of the total it can contain when saturated, at that temperature.

When air with a relative humidity of 100 per cent is cooled, some water vapor must be lost by the process of

Below: The main low clouds (below 1.5 miles) include layered stratus, heaped cumulus, stratocumulus, nimbostratus and cumulonimbus – thunder clouds. Medium clouds are altocumulus and altostratus. High clouds (above 4 miles) include cirrocumulus, cirrostratus and cirrus.

Above: Cumulonimbus clouds form when warm air rises rapidly. The air is cooled and the invisible water vapor condenses into visible water droplets.

Right: Lightning consists of huge electrical sparks in clouds. Lightning heats the air, causing thunder.

Below: When the temperature of a cloud is well below freezing point, ice crystals grow into snowflakes. Near the ground, the snowflakes may melt to form sleet or rain.

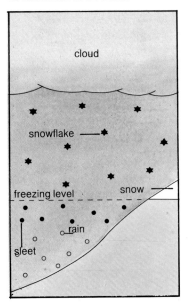

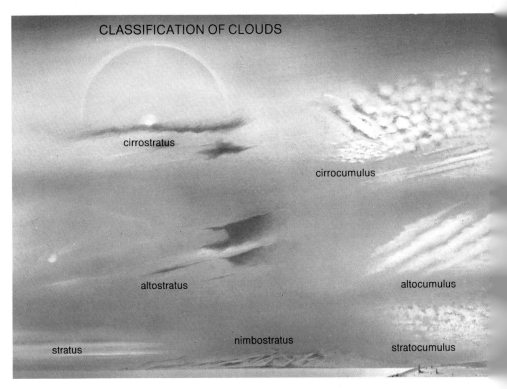

CLASSIFICATION OF CLOUDS

cirrostratus

cirrocumulus

altostratus

altocumulus

stratus

nimbostratus

stratocumulus

condensation. This means that some water vapor is turned back again into a liquid. When condensation occurs, water vapor liquefies around specks of dust or salt in the air, forming tiny but visible water droplets. A mass of these tiny droplets forms a cloud. Some clouds consist of masses of tiny ice crystals and very cold water droplets. Both are condensed at temperatures below freezing point. The water droplets may have a temperature of −15°C, but they remain liquid. However, when these *supercooled* droplets collide with ice crystals, they freeze around them.

Clouds occur in various shapes. There are two main kinds. *Cumulus* clouds are high heaps of cloud, while *stratus* clouds form in thin layers.

Precipitation

Precipitation is the general name for moisture lost from clouds. The most familiar example is rain. Rain is

Right: Three ways in which clouds are formed. Orographic clouds form when winds rise over mountains. But as the air descends again, it is warmed, and little rain falls. Thunderclouds are formed by fast-rising air currents. Frontal clouds occur in depressions, when warm air rises over cold air.

formed in several ways within clouds. In warm regions, the tiny water droplets are blown around. As they move, they hit against and merge with other droplets. Finally, the droplets become so heavy that they fall to the ground as large raindrops.

In temperate regions, where the clouds are well below freezing point, the ice crystals grow as supercooled water droplets freeze around them. When the ice crystals become large, they fall downward as snowflakes. Near the ground, they melt and become raindrops. However, if the air near the ground is cold enough, then the crystals fall as snow.

Other forms of precipitation include sleet, hail, mist, fog and frost. Sleet is a mixture of rain and snow. Hail consists of large pellets of ice. Mist and fog are masses of tiny water droplets near the ground. Frost forms when the water vapor condenses into ice crystals on chilled surfaces.

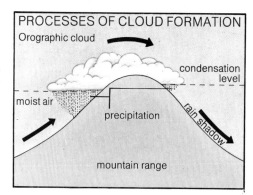

PROCESSES OF CLOUD FORMATION

Orographic cloud

condensation level

moist air

precipitation

rain shadow

mountain range

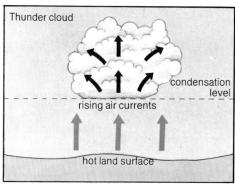

Thunder cloud

condensation level

rising air currents

hot land surface

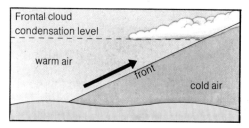

Frontal cloud
condensation level

warm air

front

cold air

cirrus

8 miles

high

4 miles

middle

cumulonimbus

1·3 miles

low

cumulus

sea level

Drifting continents

If you look at a map of the Atlantic Ocean, you will see that the east side of North and South America is a similar shape to the west side of Europe and Africa. This similarity suggests that the continents were once joined together.

Studies of the ocean floor show that coastlines are not the true edges of continents. Instead, the continents are bordered by continental shelves, which are hidden by shallow seas. Recent mapping of the oceans shows that the edges of the shelves on both sides of the Atlantic fit together even better than the coastlines.

The theory of continental drift was first put forward about 70 years ago. It was supported by much evidence of similar rock structures and fossils which occur on both sides of the Atlantic. For example, fossils of an extinct reptile named *Mesosaurus* are found in South America and Africa. The simplest way to explain why these fossils occur in widely separated places is that South America and Africa must have been joined when *Mesosaurus* was living on Earth.

Moving plates

New evidence to support continental drift came to light in studies of the oceans made in the 1950s and 1960s. Most scientists now accept the theory of *plate tectonics,* which states that the Earth's crust is split, like a cracked egg, into solid plates, and that these plates are moving around.

Scientists have discovered that the rocks in the oceans are no older than about 200 million years. This makes the oceans very young compared with the continents. The youngest rocks in the oceans are near enormous mountain ranges, called *ocean ridges.* Along these ridges, new rock is constantly being added as magma wells up from the Earth's mantle. The centers of the ocean ridges are edges of plates. As the new rock is added, the plates are pushed apart, by a process called *ocean spreading.* At the top of the mantle, some rocks may be fluid, and as they move sideways, they carry the continents with them. Studies of the deepest parts of the oceans, the ocean

trenches, show that they, too, are plate edges. However, there, one plate is being forced down beneath another. The descending plate is being melted in the mantle.

Pangaea

Scientists now believe that about 200 million years ago all the world's continents where grouped in one vast super-continent, called Pangaea. But about 180 million years ago Pangaea began to split up. The continents then drifted to their present positions.

Right: The diagram shows part of the Earth, from the Pacific Ocean to Africa. The Earth's crust includes the continental crust (brown) and the heavier, or denser, oceanic crust (green). The crust is split into rigid plates which are slowly moving.

SOUTH AMERICAN PLATE
MOVING WEST

SOUTH AMERICA

PACIFIC OCEAN

ANDES

active volcanoes fed by melting crust

Peru – Chile ocean trench

shallow earthquakes

partial melting of crust to feed volcanoes

melting crust

deepest earthquakes

continental shelf

continental slo

Above: Surtsey, a volcanic island off Iceland, is on the mid-Atlantic ridge.

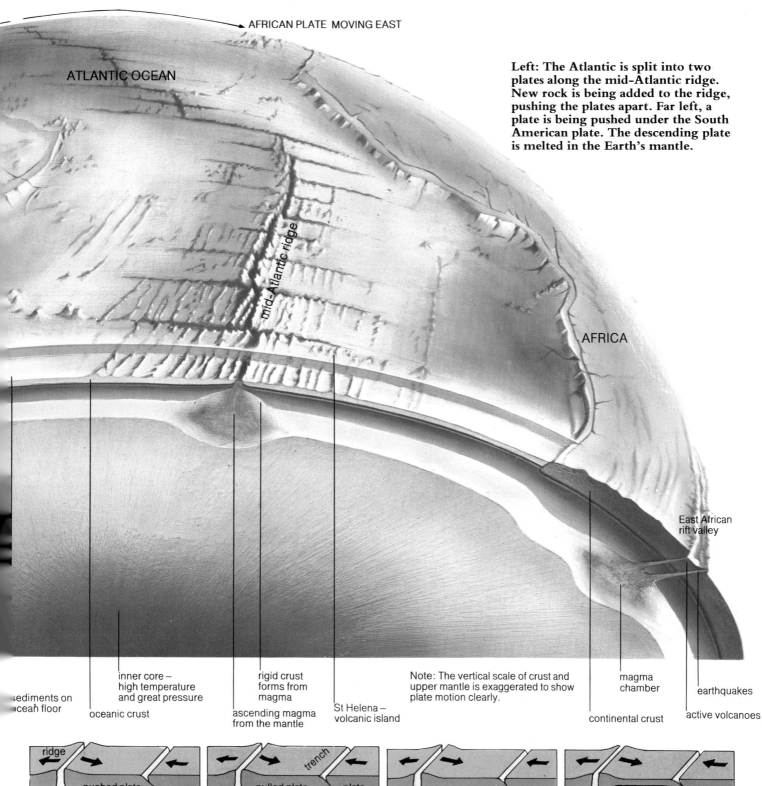

AFRICAN PLATE MOVING EAST

ATLANTIC OCEAN

mid-Atlantic ridge

AFRICA

Left: The Atlantic is split into two plates along the mid-Atlantic ridge. New rock is being added to the ridge, pushing the plates apart. Far left, a plate is being pushed under the South American plate. The descending plate is melted in the Earth's mantle.

East African rift valley

sediments on ocean floor

inner core – high temperature and great pressure

oceanic crust

rigid crust forms from magma

ascending magma from the mantle

St Helena – volcanic island

Note: The vertical scale of crust and upper mantle is exaggerated to show plate motion clearly.

magma chamber

continental crust

earthquakes

active volcanoes

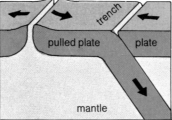
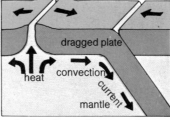
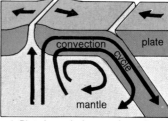
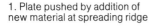

1. Plate pushed by addition of new material at spreading ridge

2. Plate pulled by weight of descending slab as it cools

3. Plate dragged by convection current in the fluid mantle

4. Plate is cooled, upper boundary of mantle convection cycle

Above: Several forces may make plates move. Diagram 1 shows magma being added to an ocean ridge. This new rock pushes the plates apart. When plates collide, one is forced beneath the other. Diagram 2 shows how the heavy descending crust may be pulling plates apart. It is also possible that parts of the upper mantle are fluid and the rocks move in convection currents(Diagram 3). Such currents may drag plates apart. Diagram 4 suggests that these currents may form continuous cycles, extending far into the mantle.

Earthquakes

Earthquakes are sudden and sometimes violent movements in the Earth's crust, which shake the land. They occur when rocks move along faults (large cracks) in the crust. Most of them occur near the edges of moving plates (see page 10).

The map on these pages shows where earthquakes have occurred around the world. Note how many of the dots are grouped in clear belts, or lines. For example, one belt winds through the Atlantic Ocean, following the center of the mid-Atlantic ridge, a plate edge. And in the Pacific Ocean earthquakes also occur near the deep ocean trenches, where one plate is being pushed beneath another. Hence, the clear belts of dots on the map roughly represent plate edges.

Transform faults

A third kind of plate edge associated with earthquakes is called a *transform fault*. This is a long crack in the surface of the crust where plates move *alongside* each other.

In California there is a transform fault 600 miles long, called the San Andreas fault. In 1906, a sudden movement occurred along this fault. Near the city of San Francisco, the plate edges moved about 15 feet. This violent jerk shook the city. Many buildings collapsed and electrical short-circuits and broken gas pipes caused many fires.

Earthquake forecasting

Millions of people have died in China as a result of earthquakes. In 1556, one earthquake killed an estimated 800,000 people.

Recently, the Chinese have been searching for ways of forecasting earthquakes. Scientists have noticed that animals behave oddly before an earthquake. Others have studied strange tilts in the ground, which appear before some earthquakes. This may show that underground rocks are being twisted. Another method is to measure the amounts of a rare gas called radon in well water. This gas is usually trapped in rocks. When the rocks crack, it escapes and is dissolved in water.

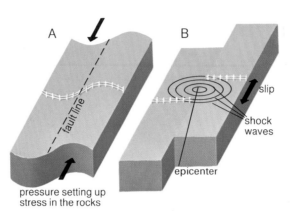

Above: Transform faults, such as the San Andreas fault in California, become jammed after an earthquake. Tension increases (A), until it is finally released in a sudden jerk (B).

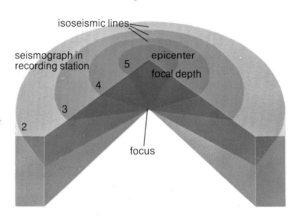

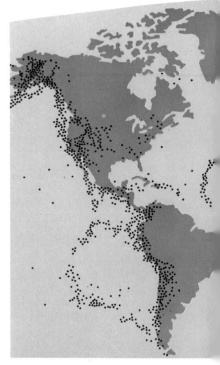

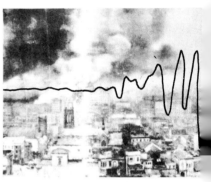

Above: The focus (point of origin) of an earthquake is underground. The point on the surface directly above the focus is called the epicenter. The distance from the focus to the epicenter is called the focal depth. Destructive earthquakes are shallow-focus, with a focal depth of less than 40 miles. Isoseismic lines join places which feel an equal intensity. The numbers show that the intensity is reduced away from the epicenter.

Top: The dots show places where earthquakes have occurred. Many are concentrated in belts, which mark the edges of plates in the Earth's crust.

Above: The picture shows the ruins of San Francisco after the famous earthquake of 1906. The seismograph record of the vibrations, shown on the photograph, were recorded in Albany, New York, which is 3020 miles away from the earthquake's focus.

The Chinese claimed a successful earthquake forecast in 1975, when all the people of the city of Haicheng were evacuated 2 hours before the city was destroyed. But earthquake forecasting is still in its infancy.

Earthquake measurement

The point of origin of an earthquake is called the *focus*. The most destructive earthquakes are *shallow-focus*. This means that they occur near the surface.

Earthquakes are recorded on instruments called *seismographs*.

The strength, or magnitude, of an earthquake is measured on the Richter scale from 1 to 9. Each successive number represents a ten-fold increase in magnitude. Earthquakes of 2 on the scale are barely noticeable, but 8 on the scale represents an extremely violent tremor. The most powerful earthquake yet measured was 8.9 on the Richter scale.

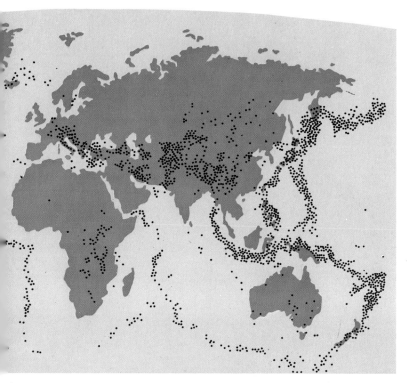

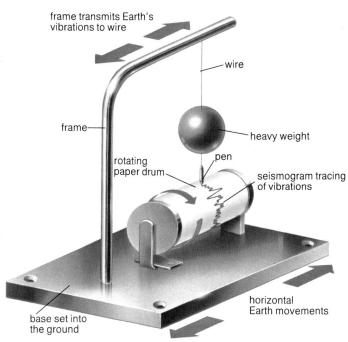

frame transmits Earth's vibrations to wire

wire

frame

heavy weight

rotating paper drum

pen

seismogram tracing of vibrations

base set into the ground

horizontal Earth movements

Above: The diagram shows a seismograph, an instrument used to detect and to record earthquakes. It consists of a spring-suspended weight, or pendulum, and a clockwork-operated rotating drum. The base is set firmly in the ground. When the ground shakes, the frame moves backward and forward. A pen on the weight marks all the movements on the paper around the drum.

Below: A railway line in Japan which was buckled by an earthquake in 1964.

Left: Damage costing millions of dollars was caused by an earthquake which hit Alaska in March 1964. This earthquake was one of the most severe ever recorded. It measured 8.9 on the Richter scale. The houses here were smashed by an enormous landslide, which was caused by the earthquake.

Volcanoes

Scientists have identified 500 or so *active* volcanoes, of which 20 to 30 erupt every year. When not erupting, these volcanoes are said to be *dormant* (sleeping). When volcanoes have not erupted for more than 25,000 years, they are described as *extinct*. However, many volcanoes that were thought to be extinct have suddenly erupted.

Volcanic eruptions

Volcanoes are essentially holes in the ground through which *magma* reaches the surface. Magma is hot, molten rock, containing various gases. Eruptions occur when the pressure in the magma chamber beneath the surface becomes so great that it must be released.

Sometimes, the pressure is released gently in *quiet eruptions*. These occur when the magma is runny and the gases can escape easily from it. Magma, known as *lava* on the surface, pours out from fissures or vents in long streams, which may reach speeds of up to 12 miles per hour. But these eruptions are not really "quiet." Sometimes, lava fire-fountains rise up to 1600 feet into the air.

When the magma is viscous (stiff) and the volcanic gases cannot easily escape, *explosive eruptions* occur. The expanding gases shatter the magma into tiny bits of ash, or larger lumps, called bombs. The ash is thrown high into the air. In the most intense explosions, much of the original cone may be destroyed. However, most volcanoes are *intermediate* in type.

Quiet eruptions produce low, *shield* volcanoes shaped like upturned saucers. Explosive eruptions produce steep cones of ash. Intermediate volcanoes usually have cones made up of layers of ash and hardened lava.

Where volcanoes occur

Most volcanoes lie near the edges of the plates in the Earth's crust. Some rise from the oceanic ridges, where new crustal rock is being formed. For example, the volcanic island of Surtsey, which appeared off Iceland in 1963, lies on the mid-Atlantic ridge. Other volcanoes lie near plate edges where one plate is being forced into

the mantle. The descending plate is melted, producing magma, which rises to the surface through volcanoes.

A few volcanoes, however, lie far from plate edges. They probably occur at "hot spots" in the Earth's mantle, where radioactive heat is creating magma. This magma rises up through the overlying plate.

Forecasting eruptions

Volcanoes can cause great destruction and loss of life. In some densely-populated areas, active volcanoes are observed by scientists. The scientists check any changes in temperature and pressure in the volcanoes. They also look out for any changes in the slope of the mountain, which they measure with tiltometers. When marked changes are discovered, they issue warnings and people are evacuated.

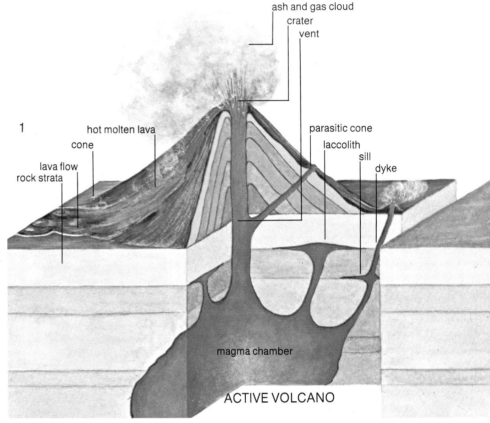

1

ash and gas cloud
crater
vent
parasitic cone
laccolith
sill
dyke
hot molten lava
cone
lava flow
rock strata
magma chamber
ACTIVE VOLCANO

Right: Krakatoa Island, Indonesia, was once a group of volcanic cones. In 1883, the largest volcanic explosion in modern times destroyed two-thirds of the island. It was heard 2940 miles away, and it generated high waves which drowned 36,000 people on nearby Java and Sumatra.

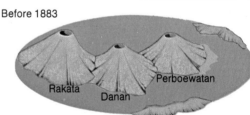

Before 1883

Rakata　Danan　Perboewatan

14

Left: In an active volcano (1), magma rises up the vent. Magma may be exploded out as fine ash, and some may emerge as lava from the vent or from side vents (parasitic cones). Other magma is forced into surrounding rocks as dykes (sheets that cut vertically across rock strata), sills (which are parallel to rock strata) and laccoliths (domes). In an extinct volcano (2), the vent is plugged by solid lava. A lake may form in the crater. Lava plugs (3) may form hills after the cone is worn away.

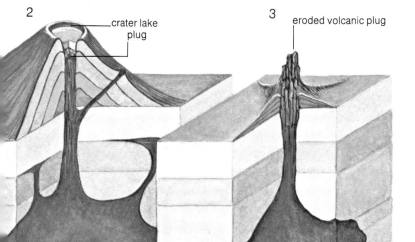

2
— crater lake
— plug

3
eroded volcanic plug

EXTINCT VOLCANO

PLUG

After 1883

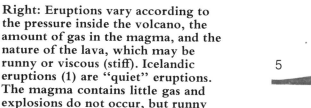

Right: Eruptions vary according to the pressure inside the volcano, the amount of gas in the magma, and the nature of the lava, which may be runny or viscous (stiff). Icelandic eruptions (1) are "quiet" eruptions. The magma contains little gas and explosions do not occur, but runny lava pours from fissures (cracks) in the ground. Hawaiian eruptions (2) are also quiet. Runny lava flows from the vent and piles up in low, shield-like volcanoes. In Strombolian eruptions (3), explosive periods occur when gas in the magma shoots ash into the air. Vulcanian eruptions (4) contain more viscous magma, whose surface hardens quickly. Gas in the magma periodically explodes bits of the hardened crust into the air. Vesuvian eruptions (5) are even more explosive and huge clouds of ash rise from the vent. Peléan eruptions (6), named after Mount Pelée in Martinique, erupt clouds of hot gas and bits of magma, which roll downhill. Plinean eruptions (7), named after the Roman writer Pliny, who recorded the eruption of Vesuvius in AD 79, are the most explosive of all. There are no lava flows. Instead, the gas-filled magma is shattered into ash which rises a mile or more into the air.

Left: The Kilauea volcano in Hawaii emits fire fountains of molten magma.

Mountain building

The four main kinds of mountains are volcanoes (described on pages 14–15), fold mountains, block mountains and intrusive mountains. Most mountains were formed by forces associated with plate movements in the Earth's crust (see pages 10–11).

Fold mountains

Fold mountains form the world's most extensive ranges, including the Alps, Andes, Appalachians, Himalayas and Rockies. All these ranges were formed by plates pushing against each other.

For example, the Himalayas are a fairly recent fold mountain range. Their history begins about 180 million years ago. This was when the ancient super-continent of Pangaea began to break up (see pages 10–11). At that time, the land that forms present-day India lay a long way from Asia. It was sandwiched between south-eastern Africa and Antarctica and a huge ocean, called the Tethys Sea, lay between it and Asia. As Pangaea broke up, the Indian plate began to move away from Africa and Antarctica and to drift slowly toward Asia.

Around 50 million years ago, the Indian plate was starting to push against the Asian one. As it moved forward, the level rock strata and sediments on the bed of the Tethys Sea were squeezed together and folded upward into large loops. In time, the Tethys Sea vanished and the folded rocks formed the Himalayas which now join the Indian and Asian plates.

The enormous pressure between the plates greatly compressed the rocks in the Himalayas. The folding explains why fossils of sea creatures are often found near the tops of the highest mountains.

Block mountains

Pressure and tension caused by plate movements sometimes produce fractures (cracks) in rocks, forming huge faults.

Tugging movements make some blocks of land slip down along faults. Other blocks are raised up along faults, producing steep slopes called fault scarps. Such uplifted blocks of land are called block mountains.

Above: Mount Fuji, in Japan, is a volcano which last erupted in 1707. It is Japan's highest peak and towers 12,388 feet above sea level. Many Japanese regard it as a sacred mountain, and every summer pilgrims climb to the top. Volcanoes are one of the four main kinds of mountains. Diagram 1, above right, shows how the vent has cut through existing rock strata, and magma (in the forms of ash and lava) accumulates in layers to form a volcanic cone.

Below: Half Dome, in Yosemite National Park, in California, is an intrusive mountain. This spectacular peak, a mountaineer's delight, consists of hard granite. It was formed from magma which cooled and solidified underground. Diagram 4, below right, shows how intrusive granite resists erosion, while the softer rocks around it are worn away.

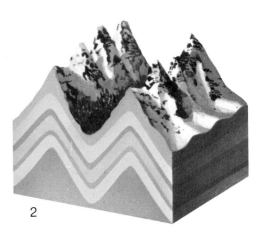

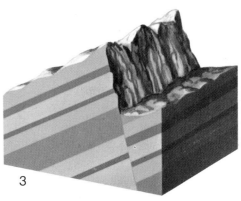

TYPES OF FOLDS

flat lying strata

symmetrical

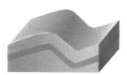
asymmetrical

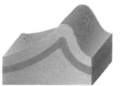
overturned

isoclinal series

recumbent

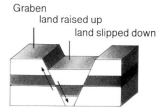
Graben
land raised up
land slipped down

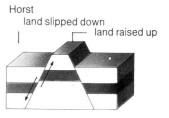
Horst
land slipped down
land raised up

Above: The Himalayan mountains of Asia are the world's highest. The Himalayas are fold mountains, like those shown in diagram 2, left. They were formed by tremendous lateral (sideways) pressure, which squeezed up formerly level rock strata into great loops, or folds. Some kinds of folds are shown at the top of the page.

Below: The Sierra Nevadas, in California, are a mountain range which was created when a block of land was pushed upward along a fault. This produced a slope, called a fault scarp, which rises steeply above the land on the other side of the fault. Diagram 3, left, shows that when blocks of land are pushed upward the rocks are displaced, such that the rock strata on one side of the fault do not match with the rock strata on the other side. Such raised land areas are called block mountains.

Above right: The two diagrams show how two features called graben and horsts are formed by Earth movements. Graben, or rift valleys, are created when a block of land sinks down between two roughly parallel faults, creating a steep-sided trough. Horsts, or block mountains, are produced by a movement in the opposite direction, that is, when the central block is pushed upward between the parallel faults.

Such movements occurred in eastern Africa. Huge blocks of land sank down between long faults to form the East African rift valley, the world's largest rift valley. Uplifting raised up the Ruwenzori range, a block mountain bordering the rift valley.

Intrusive mountains

The magma which comes out of volcanoes hardens into rocks called *extrusive rocks,* because the material has been *extruded,* or pushed out, onto the surface. However, much magma never reaches the surface. Instead, it is *intruded,* or is forced into, existing rock strata underground. Enormous bodies of intrusive magma, called *laccoliths* and *batholiths,* may bend overlying rock strata upward into domes. When the magma cools, it forms such tough intrusive rocks as granite. Eventually, the softer, overlying rocks are worn away. The granite is then exposed on the surface, forming an intrusive mountain. The Black Hills of South Dakota, are an example of mountains formed in this way.

The power of the sea

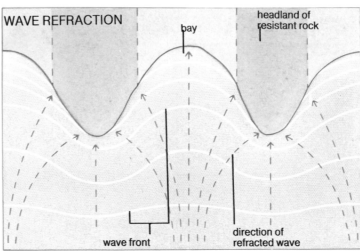

On January 31, 1953, a combination of high tides and storm winds, reaching 50 miles per hour, raised the level of the North Sea to heights not known before. During the night, huge waves smashed many holes in the dikes (sea walls) of the Netherlands, and the sea flooded more than four per cent of the country. That same night, the coast of eastern England was severely battered by the waves. In one place, where the rocks consisted of loose glacial deposits, 88 feet of land were ripped away in 2 hours.

The power of the sea is, in fact, responsible for the varying coastal scenery we see around land areas. The sea has the power to erode, transport and deposit material.

Erosion by the sea

The sea can wear away the land in several ways. First, it can dissolve some rocks. Second, waves can trap air in cracks in coastal rocks. The trapped air is compressed, but when the pressure is released, the air expands explosively, making the cracks larger or breaking off lumps of rock. Third, storm waves can carry loose pebbles and rocks. When this loose material is hurled at the shore, it hollows out caves and undercuts cliffs. Finally, the restless sea rubs loose rocks against each other, wearing them down into smaller and smaller pieces. This process creates the sand and rounded pebbles we find on beaches.

Wave erosion occurs most quickly in areas where the rocks offer the least resistance. For example, bays form when softer rocks are worn back faster than nearby hard rocks, which remain as headlands. But even headlands are finally removed. This happens when waves cut caves in the sides of the headlands. The caves meet to form natural *arches*. When the arches collapse, rocky pillars, called *stacks,* arc left behind on the seaward side. They, too, are eventually cut down by the pounding waves.

Transport and deposition

Waves and currents move loose sand and pebbles along coasts by *long-shore*

Above: The diagram shows two headlands formed from resistant rocks, enclosing a bay. The directions of the waves are shown by the arrows. As the wave front approaches land, the wave directions change according to the shape of the land, because waves tend to reach the shore roughly at right angles. The bending of wave directions is called wave refraction.

Below left: The diagram shows a typical coastline in the North Atlantic, which is being steadily worn back by wave action. At low tide, the water level is well below the cliff. But, at high tide, the water extends right up to the cliff. Storm waves hurl loose rocks at the base of the cliff and undercut it. Finally, slabs of rock crash down and the cliff retreats.

WAVE REFRACTION

bay — headland of resistant rock

wave front — direction of refracted wave

NORTH ATLANTIC TYPE PLATFORM

cliff

high tide

low tide

shore platform

undercutting leads to cliff collapse

beach material

drift (see diagram on page 19). This movement of material is interrupted when the coastline changes direction, such as at bays or river estuaries. At such places, the material is dropped and piles up in ridges called *spits*. Sometimes, spits extend right across a bay: Such spits are called *baymouth bars*. Some bars are not linked to land. Instead, the material piles up offshore in long ridges. Another kind of spit is called a *tombolo*. Tombolos link islands to the mainland, forming a natural bridge, such as Chesil Beach in Dorset, England.

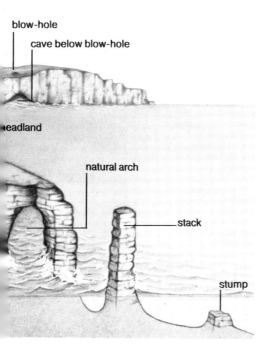

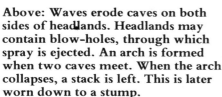

blow-hole
cave below blow-hole
headland
natural arch
stack
stump

Above: Waves erode caves on both sides of headlands. Headlands may contain blow-holes, through which spray is ejected. An arch is formed when two caves meet. When the arch collapses, a stack is left. This is later worn down to a stump.

Below: These natural arches are on the coast of the Algarve, in Portugal.

Above: A former island in the Scottish sea-loch Eriboll is now joined to the mainland by a low ridge of sand and shingle, called a tombolo. It consists of material worn away from another part of the coast and carried here by waves and currents. Tombolo, an Italian word, comes from the name of two land bridges, linking the former island of Monte Argentario to Italy.

Below: The process by which waves move pebbles and sand along a beach is called long-shore drift. It occurs when the wind direction and the wave front approach the beach at an angle. The advance of water up the beach, called the swash, is also at an angle. But the backwash is at right angles to the beach. Hence, material is moved up the coast in a zig-zag direction.

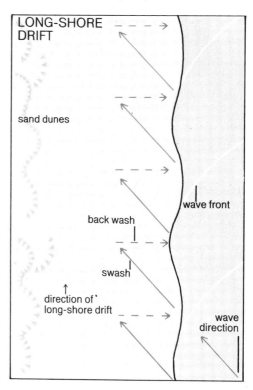

LONG-SHORE DRIFT

sand dunes

wave front

back wash

swash

direction of long-shore drift

wave direction

Left: Miami Beach in south-eastern Florida is a tourist center with beautiful beaches. Groynes, which are low walls or jetties, have been built into the sea to protect the beach from wave erosion. The groynes trap the sand and prevent its removal by long-shore drift.

The ocean depths

The oceans cover about 71 per cent of the Earth's surface. The three main oceans are the Pacific, whose area of over 64 million square miles is greater than the areas of all the continents combined; the Atlantic Ocean; and the Indian Ocean. The Arctic and Antarctic oceans around the poles are really just extensions of the three main oceans.

Until recently, little was known about the ocean bed. In the last 30 years, however, mapping by echo-sounders has greatly increased our knowledge. And since the 1930s scientists have begun to explore the dark waters of the ocean depths in craft called bathyspheres and bathyscaphes. The record descent (35,480 feet) was made by the bathyscaphe *Trieste* in 1960.

Features of the ocean floor

The average depth of the oceans is about 11,400 feet. The deepest point, in the Marianas Trench in the Pacific Ocean, is 35,857 feet below the surface. The ocean trenches are places where one plate is being pushed down beneath another (see pages 10–11).

Other plate edges in the oceans are in the centers of the oceanic ridges, where new rock is being formed from

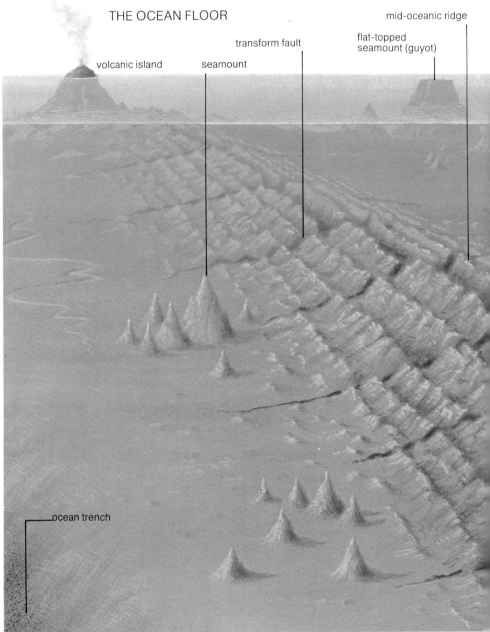

THE OCEAN FLOOR

volcanic island · seamount · transform fault · mid-oceanic ridge · flat-topped seamount (guyot) · ocean trench

Above: The ocean depths are as varied as the land. There are deep ocean trenches, seamounts, enormous oceanic ridges which contain central rift valleys, volcanic islands which rise from the ocean floor, and deep submarine (underwater) canyons, which may have been scoured out by strong muddy currents, called submarine density currents.

Left: Ocean research ships carry many instruments. This probe measures the temperatures and salinity (saltiness) of ocean water.

Right: Seen from a point over Tahiti, in the Pacific Ocean, our planet appears almost completely covered by water.

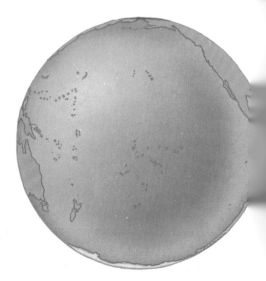

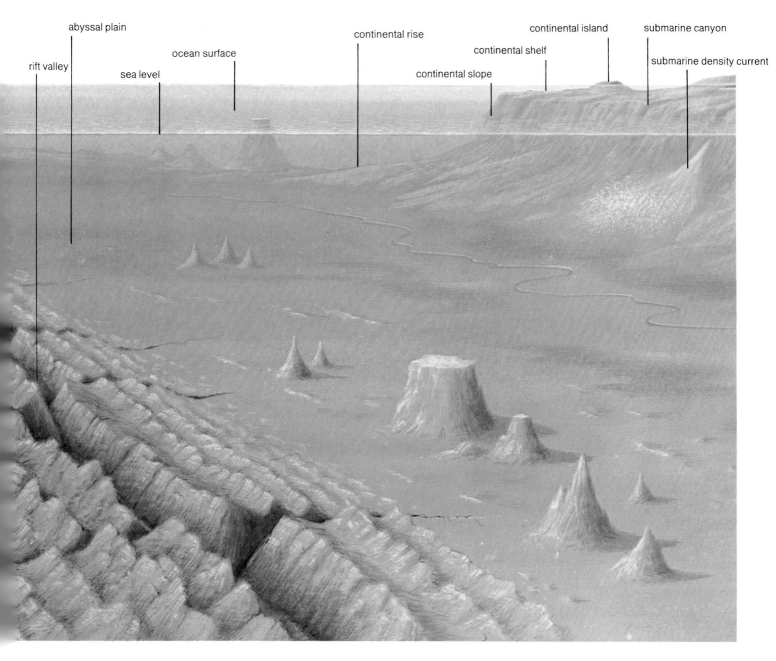

rift valley

abyssal plain

sea level

ocean surface

continental rise

continental slope

continental shelf

continental island

submarine canyon

submarine density current

Below: Echo-sounders measure the depth of water by beaming sound waves to the ocean bed and recording the time taken for their echoes to return. Seismic surveys investigate the rock strata under the ocean bed.

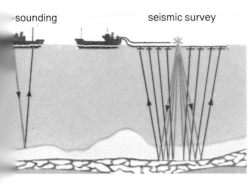

sounding   seismic survey

magma in the central rift valleys. The largest oceanic ridge is in the Atlantic. It is 10,000 miles long and 500 miles wide. Its highest peak is Mount Pico in the Azores, which rises 23,393 feet from the ocean floor. Beyond the ridges are flat *abyssal plains* and, in some places, *abyssal hills*.

Rising from the abyssal plains are isolated mountains called *seamounts*. The world's highest mountain, measured from its base, is Mauna Kea, a volcano on the island of Hawaii in the Pacific Ocean. Mauna Kea is 13,666 feet above sea level, but another 19,495 feet are hidden from view.

This gives Mauna Kea a total height of 33,161 feet.

Around most continents are gently sloping *continental shelves*. At the edge of these shelves are the steep *continental slopes*. At the bottom of these slopes are the more gently sloping *continental rises*. These are composed of sediments brought from the land by muddy underwater currents, called *submarine density currents*. Some continental slopes are cut by deep canyons, which may have been worn out by the submarine density currents, such as the one formed by the muddy water of the Zaire River in Africa.

The world of minerals

The Earth's crust basically consists of *elements*. These are substances which cannot be broken down into other substances by chemical means. The chief elements in the crust are oxygen and silicon, which together make up 74.32 per cent of the crust's weight; aluminium, iron, calcium, sodium, potassium and magnesium make up 24.27 per cent. Another 84 elements occur naturally in the crust, making up the other 1.41 per cent.

Minerals and rocks

Some elements, such as gold, silver and copper, sometimes occur in the crust in a pure or nearly pure state. They are minerals, called *native elements*. But most minerals are a combination of elements.

Most minerals have a definite chemical formula and are *homogeneous*; that is, any part of the mineral is the same as any other part. Halite (salt) has the formula NaCl, which means that it is a combination of equal parts of two elements, sodium (Na) and chlorine (Cl). Nearly 3000 minerals have been identified. Some of these are common rock-forming minerals, while others are rare.

Rocks consist of minerals. But rocks are *heterogeneous*; that is, the

Right: The diagram shows places where minerals are found. When magma cools, the minerals crystallize to form such rocks as granite (1). Granite consists of such common rock-forming minerals as quartz, feldspar and mica. After granite has formed, some molten rock containing rarer minerals may be left over. These crystallize separately. Minerals also form in cavities, such as sheet-like veins and geodes (round lumps). Minerals worn from rocks may collect in river beds (2). Some minerals form when pressure, heat and gases (from the magma) metamorphose (alter) such rocks as limestone (3) and shale (4). Hydrothermal veins (5) form when hot, mineral-rich fluids are injected into existing rocks. These veins are major sources of valuable minerals. Beach deposits (6) often contain good mineral specimens. Ancient metamorphic rocks (7) may be sources of some rare minerals. Some sedimentary rocks (8), for example rock salt, consist largely of one mineral.

Above: Granite is a rock. It consists of several minerals.

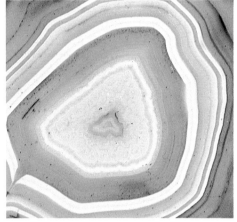

Above: Agate is a banded mineral which is a form of chalcedony.

Below: Gold is an element which occurs in a pure state as a mineral.

Below: Quartz is a common mineral which occurs in several colors.

HOW AND WHERE MINERALS OCCUR ① ② ③ ④ ⑤

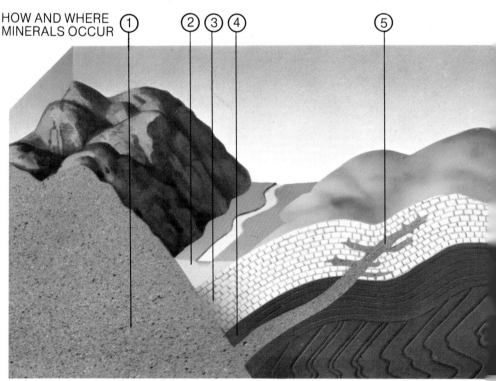

22

Left: Varieties of the fairly common, hard mineral corundum, shown here, include two rare and highly prized stones: the transparent red ruby and the blue sapphire. Green, violet, brown and yellow varieties also occur, but the commonest form is dull-looking. It is used as an abrasive.

Below: Crowns, scepters and other insignia have traditionally symbolized power and status. Precious metals, such as gold and silver, and rare gemstones, especially diamonds, rubies, sapphires and emeralds, are used in the British royal insignia.

Below: Diamond, the purest form of carbon, is the hardest mineral. After skillful cutting and polishing, it reflects light, producing a play of colors, called fire.

amounts of minerals in a rock vary from sample to sample. There are three kinds of rocks. *Igneous rocks* form from magma. Many *sedimentary rocks* form from fragments of other rocks, such as sandstone, which forms from sand. Some are the result of chemical action, such as rock salt, which forms when sea water evaporates. Others, like coal, are organic, being formed from once-living matter. *Metamorphic rocks* are rocks that have been changed by great pressure or heat or by gases released from bodies of magma.

Properties of minerals

When magma cools, most of the minerals in the mixture crystallize (form into crystals). Nearly all minerals have a definite crystal form. But in most igneous rocks the crystals are packed together and are distorted. Well-formed crystals occur in such

places as veins and other rock cavities. Crystal forms are often used as a way of identifying minerals.

Another property of minerals is their hardness. Diamond, a form of pure carbon, is the hardest of all minerals, but you can crush talcite with your fingers. Some minerals, such as blue azurite, are always the same color but many others occur in several colors.

Another property is specific gravity. This is the ratio between the weight of a mineral and the weight of an equal volume of water. Other features are cleavage (the way minerals split when struck), optical properties (how they reflect, transmit or absorb light), and streak (the color of the powdered mineral). But minerals are usually classified according to their chemical composition. Groups include oxides, silicates, sulphides, and so on.

Coal

Coal, oil and natural gas are *fossil fuels,* which were formed from the remains of once-living organisms. They are not minerals, because minerals are *inorganic* (lifeless) substances.

In the last 40 years, the importance of coal as a fuel has declined because of competition with oil and natural gas. But experts estimate that the known reserves of oil will run out in the next 30 years or so, while coal reserves will last for at least 450 years. Hence, coal may soon regain its importance. Besides being a fuel, coal has many other uses. It is used to smelt metals and to make dyes, explosives, synthetic rubber and plastics in the chemical industry.

The formation of coal

When plants die, they usually decay rapidly and the once-living matter is converted by bacteria into water, carbon dioxide and salts. The process of decay is halted when plants are buried quickly in swamps or bogs, and so the partly rotted plants pile up in layers. These layers are compacted into *carbonaceous rocks,* that is, rocks composed mostly of carbon.

The first stage in coal formation can be seen in some soggy moorlands, marshes and shallow lakes. There, the decaying plants form *peat,* a light brown substance. Peat may be cut for fuel, but first it must be dried, because up to 90 per cent of its weight is water. Dry peat contains up to 60 per cent carbon. The second stage in coal formation is *lignite* (brown coal), which is similar to peat but much more compact. It contains 60 to 75 per cent carbon when dry. It is used as a fuel and also in the chemical industry. *Bituminous,* or household, coal is hard and contains up to 90 per cent carbon. *Anthracite,* the last stage in coal formation, contains 95 per cent carbon. This shiny, black rock is clean to handle.

Right: This diagram of a typical coal mine shows the great amount of planning and costly machinery which is needed to extract coal from deep coal seams. Inset is a miner working at the coal face. But modern mining is becoming increasingly mechanized.

Above: A reconstruction of a coal-forming forest in the Carboniferous period (345 to 280 million years ago) shows the luxuriant vegetation.

fan-house, with powerful fan to extract the foul air

The top of the upcast shaft is housed in a sealed building. This insures that the fan operates efficiently in removing used air from the whole underground area.

Other rock strata. The diagram is not to scale; these strata may be several miles deep.

The upcast shaft is used to bring coal, loaded in buckets called skips, to the surface.

A cut-away section through the unmined coal shows the machinery used in mining. The arrow shows the direction of mining into the coal face.

Room and pillar mining usually extracts only half the coal, leaving columns to support the roof.

underground railway

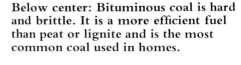

Left: Peat is the first stage in the formation of coal. In this area of Scotland, peat is forming from dead trees, heather and mosses. Dried peat is cut and used as a fuel.

Below: Soft, dark brown lignite is the second stage in coal formation.

Below center: Bituminous coal is hard and brittle. It is a more efficient fuel than peat or lignite and is the most common coal used in homes.

Below right: Anthracite is the final stage in coal formation. It is hard, shiny and black.

lignite

bituminous

anthracite

The headgear of the downcast shaft is made of an open lattice of steel girders, so that fresh air can enter to ventilate the mine.

The downcast shaft is fitted with a cage, used to convey men and equipment into and out of the mine.

coal seams

Water seepage is collected in sumps and pumped out.

conveyor belts

Above: Dark coal seams are exposed in this cliff in Antarctica. Coal has formed from the remains of ancient plants which grew in swamps. The presence of coal in Antarctica shows that this continent once had a warm climate and was situated much closer to the equator than it is today.

Most of the bituminous coal and anthracite mined today was formed around 300 million years ago. At that time, luxuriant forests with tall trees, giant ferns, mosses and horsetails grew in swamps. Many of these forests were near the coast. Periodically, the swamps were submerged, and eroded material from the land, such as sand and mud, was spread over the layers of plants. Later, the land rose and

forests grew again. As a result, coal *seams* or *beds* alternate with layers of other rocks. A sequence of coal seams and other rock layers is called a *coal measure*. This may be 4900 feet or more thick and contain 20 to 30 coal seams, between a few inches and 95 feet or more thick.

Coal mining

Some coal seams lie on or near the surface. In seams like these, coal is removed by open-cast mining. Other seams are very much deeper, and tunnels have to be cut in order to reach the coal. In most modern mines, the coal is cut by machines and hauled back from the coal face by means of conveyor belts.

Oil and natural gas

Oil and natural gas are fossil fuels extracted from the Earth's crust. They may occur together or separately. These fuels now supply more than half of the energy that is consumed in the modern world. And oil, besides being used to make gasoline, fuel oils and lubricating oils, is also important in the chemical industry, where it is used to make such things as detergents, drugs, explosives and plastics.

However, oil and natural gas take millions of years to form, and when the reserves are used up, they cannot be replaced. Experts estimate that, at the current rate of consumption, the known reserves will run out in about 30 years' time. Many nations are now reducing their consumption in order to conserve these dwindling resources.

Formation of oil and gas

Most scientists believe that oil and gas were formed from the remains of tiny animals and plants, which settled on sea and lake beds. These remains were partly changed by bacteria and then buried by thick layers of sediment. Many were buried in clays, which were compacted by pressure into rocks called *shales*. Pressure and heat also acted on the organic material, turning it into oil or gas (mainly methane). The light oil and gas were squeezed out of the shales and they flowed upwards into *permeable* rocks.

Permeable rocks may be *porous*, like sandstone, which contains tiny spaces (pores) between the grains, through which oil, gas and water can flow. Other permeable rocks, like limestone, do not have pores, but they contain many cracks through which liquids and gases can pass.

Much oil and gas, often overlying water, is found in underground reservoirs. For a large reservoir to form, the oil and gas must be trapped by *impervious rocks*, through which they cannot escape. The commonest kind of reservoir is an *anticline* (upfold), where an arched permeable rock layer is enclosed, above and below, by layers of impervious rocks. Others occur in *fault traps* or around *salt plugs* (see the diagrams at the top of this page).

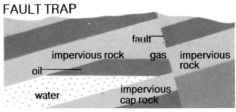

FAULT TRAP

fault
impervious rock   gas   impervious rock
oil
water   impervious cap rock

SALTDOME

impervious cap rock
water   salt plug   gas
oil
water

Above: Two rock structures in which oil and natural gas may be found. In the fault trap, left, the porous rock containing the gas and oil is enclosed by impervious rocks. Oil and gas may also be trapped around the tops of salt plugs, right.

Below: A diagram showing an oil production platform in the sea. Many oil fields are found in lakes or shallow seas. Inset is a diagram of an anticline (upfold). Oil and gas are trapped in the arched porous rock layer which is between two impervious layers.

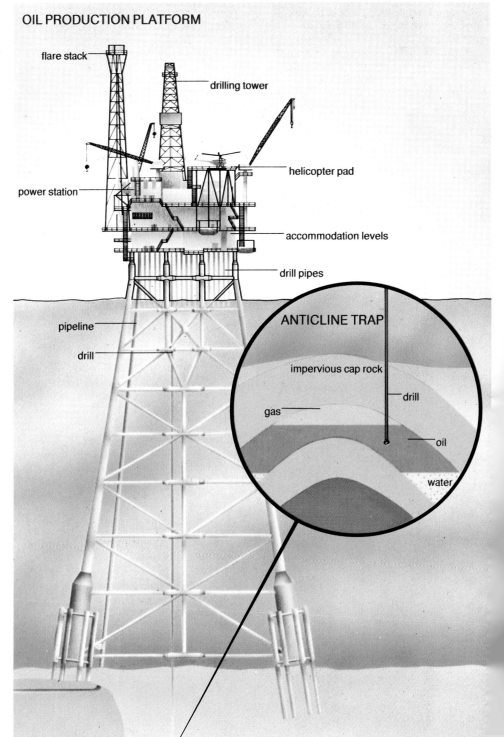

OIL PRODUCTION PLATFORM

flare stack
drilling tower
helicopter pad
power station
accommodation levels
drill pipes
pipeline
drill

ANTICLINE TRAP
impervious cap rock
drill
gas
oil
water

Prospecting and extraction

To find oil and gas, geologists must first look for promising rock structures. Underground rocks can be investigated by *seismic surveys* (see diagram, page 21). These surveys involve setting off small explosions in the ground, which generate seismic (shock) waves in the Earth's crust. By measuring the passage of the waves, the rock structures can be deduced. Other methods include aeromagnetic surveys and measurements of local variations in gravity.

When promising rock structures are found, an exploratory drilling is made. These drill-holes may reach 19,500 feet or more into the ground. When a reservoir is located, the oil and gas may rise under pressure or it may have to be pumped to the surface. It is then transported to oil refineries.

Below: This drilling rig is used to discover whether oil and natural gas are below. Mud is pumped down the drill shaft to lubricate the drill bit (cutting tool). The mud may disappear, being absorbed by porous rocks. The presence of porous rocks means that oil may be present.

Above: Natural gas is burned off at an oil field in Abu Dhabi, near the Persian Gulf. The oil is extracted after the gas has been removed. The burning of gas is wasteful. It is done, however, because of the very high cost of transporting gas to markets which are long distances away.

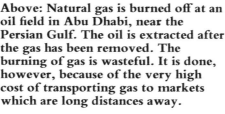

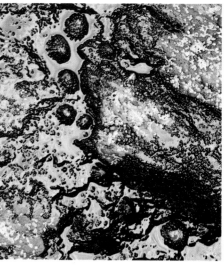

Above: A 200-mile-long gas pipeline conveys a natural gas from an inland gasfield to a processing plant on the coast of Oman, in the Middle East. In many countries, the natural gas, which overlies large oil deposits, is burned off (see top picture) so that the oil can be easily extracted.

Above right: An oil refinery on the Isle of Grain, in southeastern England, processes imported oil.

Right: Oil spillages from tankers have threatened the environment in recent years. Scientists have been seeking ways of controlling oil pollution and reducing its effects on marine life and coastal regions.

Records in the rocks

Fossils are evidence of ancient life on Earth, ranging from the footprints of dinosaurs to the carcasses of woolly mammoths preserved in the frozen soil of Siberia. But the soft parts of plants and animals are rarely fossilized, because they decay quickly after the organisms die.

Kinds of fossils

The most important condition for fossil formation is fast burial. This usually occurs when dead organisms are buried by mud or sand in the beds of seas, rivers and lakes. For example, when shells or other hard parts of organisms are buried, they are often dissolved away by water seeping through the sediments. This leaves hollows, or *molds*. Molds are often filled by minerals so that a *cast* of the original is formed. Molds and casts are common fossils. They reveal the outer shape of the organism, but not its internal structure. Sometimes, organisms are dissolved very slowly and minerals replace the molecules of the original organism one by one. As a result, the organisms are *petrified* (turned to stone). Petrified logs even show the annual rings in the wood.

Soft organisms, such as worms or leaves, are sometimes turned into thin films of carbon, called *carbon smears*. *Trace fossils* include footprints made in soft mud which was baked hard by the Sun before being buried, eggs, animal droppings and burrows.

Insects were sometimes trapped in sticky resin from trees and they were preserved when the resin hardened into *amber*. The frozen mammoths of Siberia are extremely unusual fossils, because their flesh has been preserved. They probably drowned in swamps which later froze, preserving their bodies in a natural freezer.

Most fossils occur in sedimentary rocks, which cover three-quarters of the Earth's land area. Some distorted fossils appear in metamorphic (altered) rocks, but you will not find any fossils in igneous rocks.

The meaning of fossils

The earliest fossils date back about 3 billion years. They are fossils of

GEOLOGICAL TIME SCALE

0 million years ago
2
Quaternary
Tertiary
65
Cretaceous
135
Jurassic
193
Triassic
225
Permian
280
Carboniferous
345
Devonian
395
Silurian
435
Ordovician
500
Cambrian
570
Pre-Cambrian

lobster *Crustacea*

crinoid *Echinoderm*

lepidodendron

brachiopod

trilobite

Left: The geological time scale shows the periods in the last 570 million years, with some typical fossils: a trilobite (an extinct arthropod); brachiopods (shellfish); a lepidodendron (a club moss); a crinoid (sea lily); and parts of a lobster.

Below: Jurassic ammonites. These extinct animals are related to squids.